Calming & Relaxing, Stress Relieving Adult Coloring Book

Featuring: Mandalas, Flowers & Symmetry

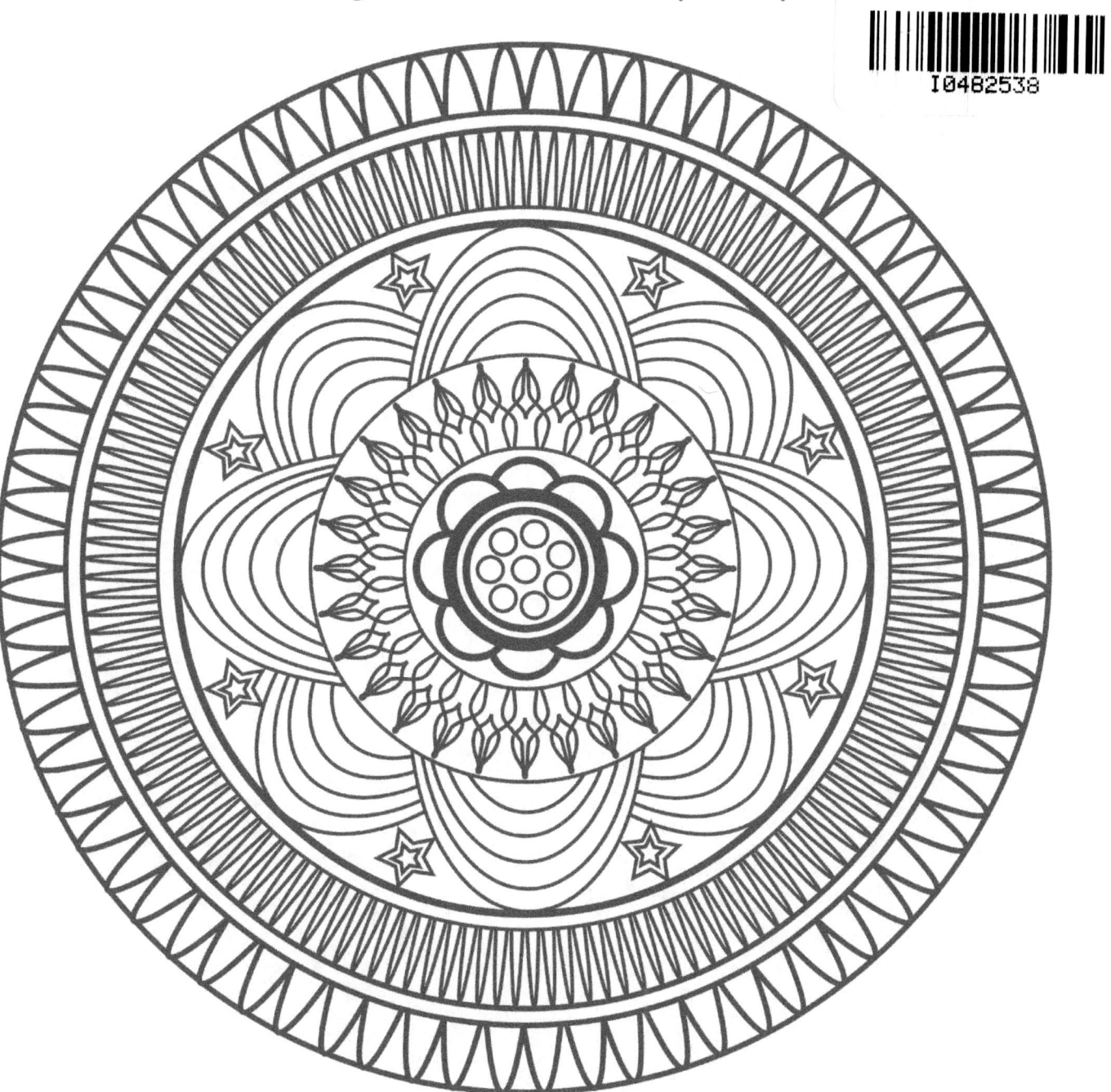

Illustrated by Lisa Higgins

Published in 2016 by
Lisa Higgins Published Collection
Perth, Western Australia
www.misshiggspublishedcollection.com

1st Edition 2016

ISBN:
ISBN-13: 978 1533337023
ISBN-10: 1533337020

Printed by Create Space

Designs by Lisa Higgins in collaboration with www.freepik.com

DEDICATION

This book is dedicated to
my beautiful Ethan and Sophie,
you inspire me in so many ways.

Welcome...

Welcome to Calming & Relaxing Stress Relieving Adult Coloring Book, each illustration has been crafted for your enjoyment featuring a variety of flowers, symmetrical patters and mandalas.

Directions

A test page has been included at the front of the book for you to test your markers for color or bleed. We would also recommend inserting a blank sheet of paper behind the page you are working on. Each illustration has been printed on a single page to ensure you are not ruining another image behind it with any marker bleeding, alternatively if you choose to frame the work at a later date you don't have to choose between your images.

I hope you enjoy this collection.

WOULD YOU LIKE AN ADULT COLORING IN PRINTABLE?

Please visit www.misshiggspublishedcollection.com and subscribe to our weekly newsletter to receive your free adult coloring in printables.

Test Page

Use this test page before coloring your illustrations.

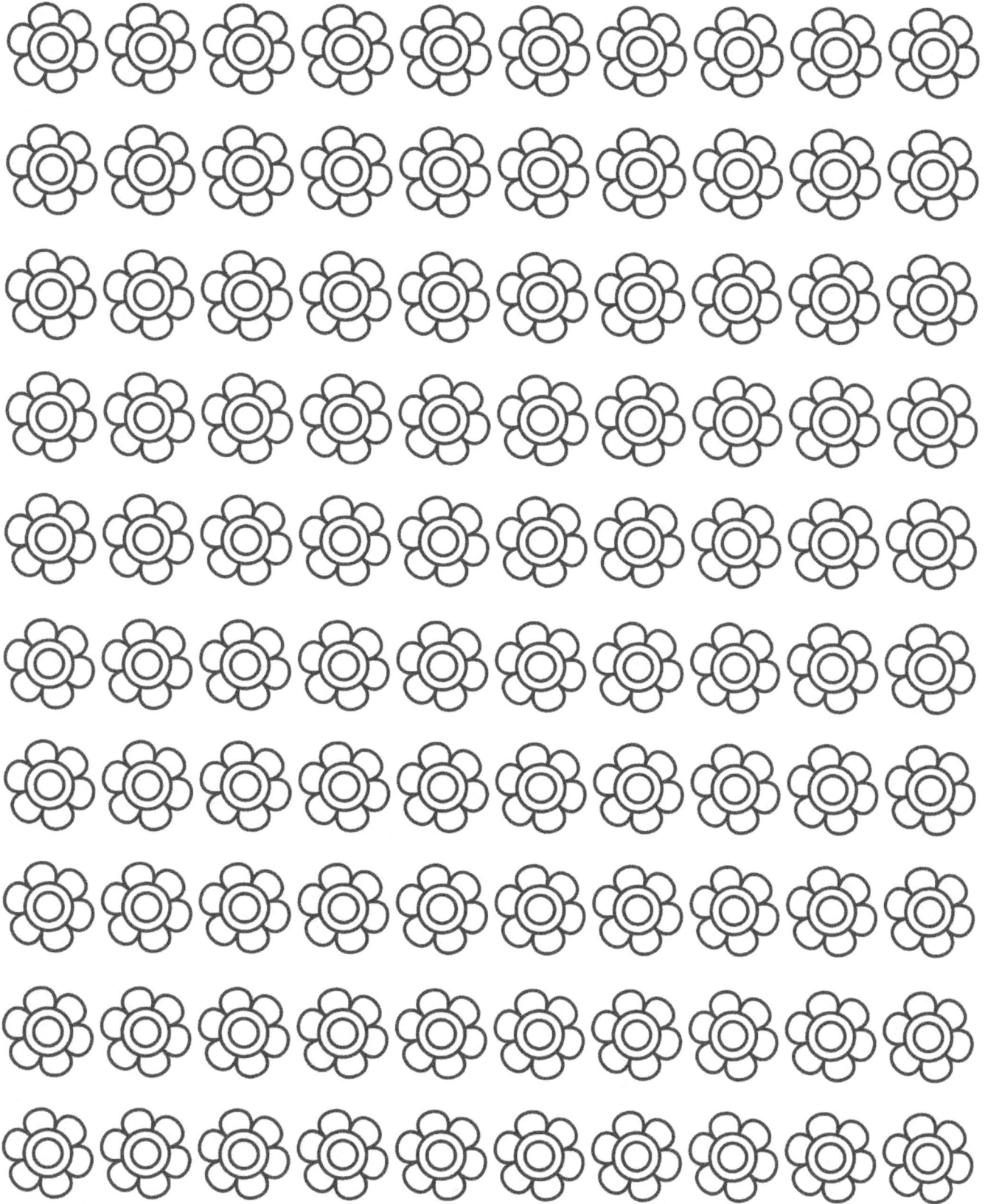

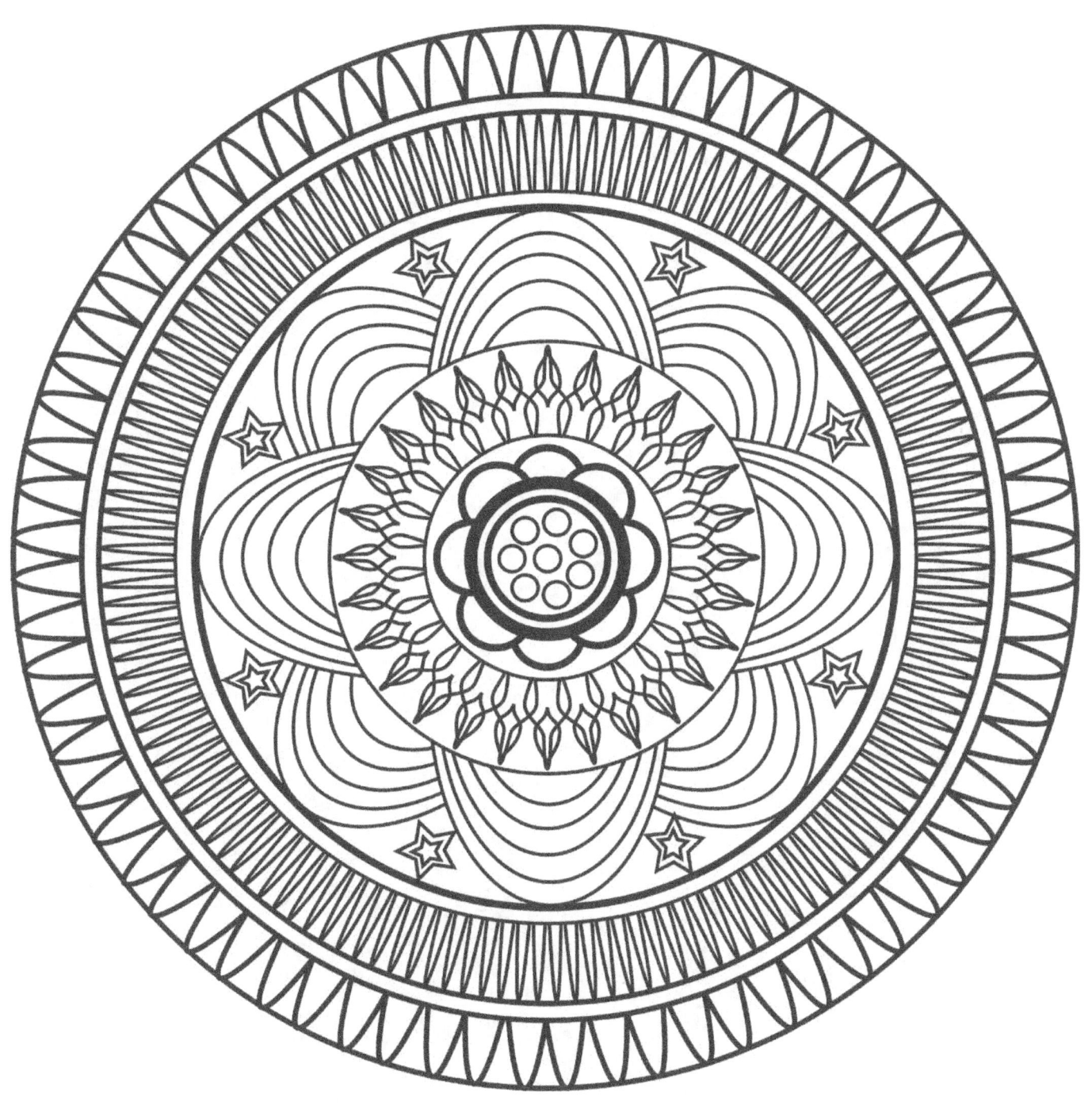

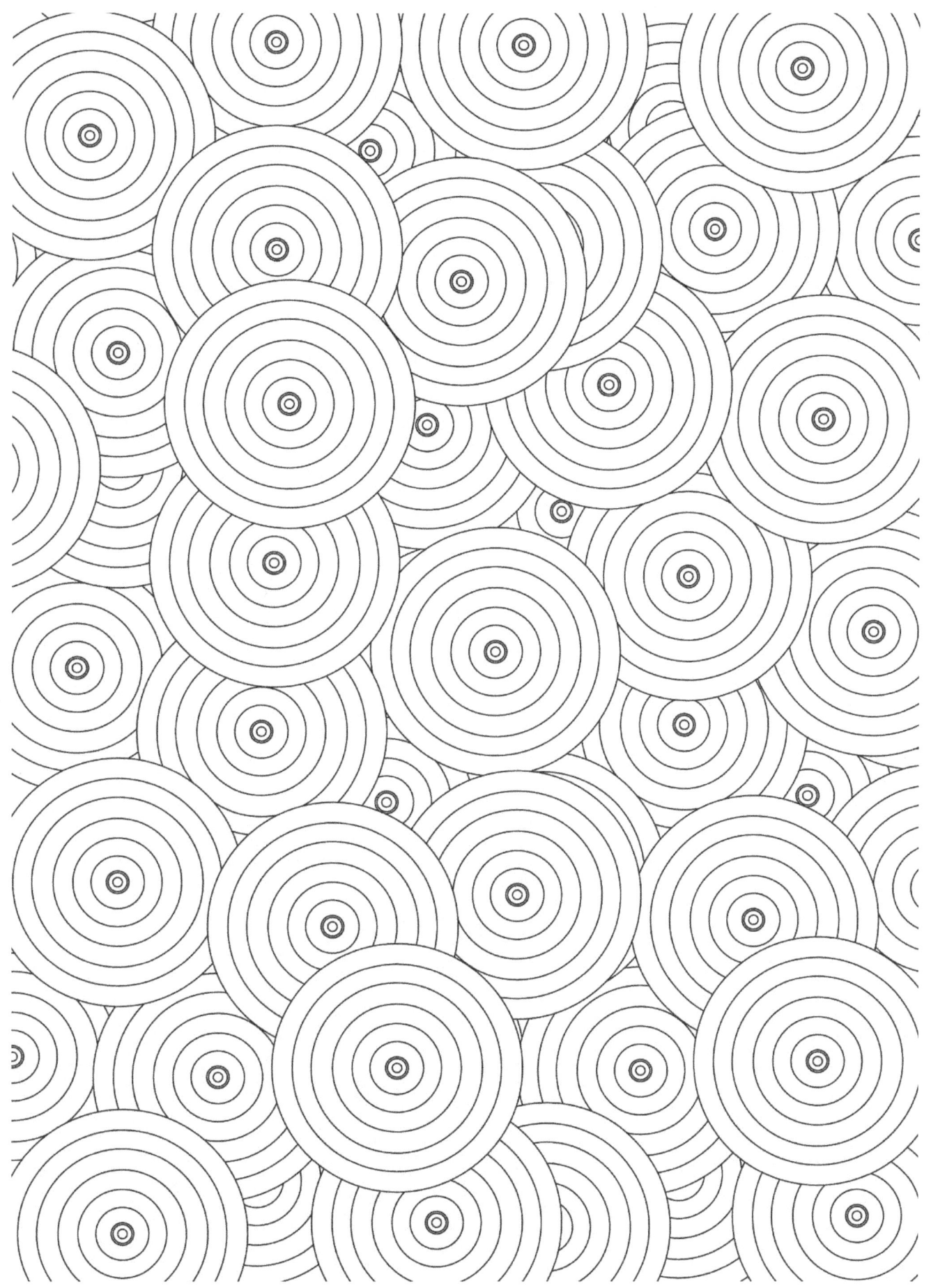

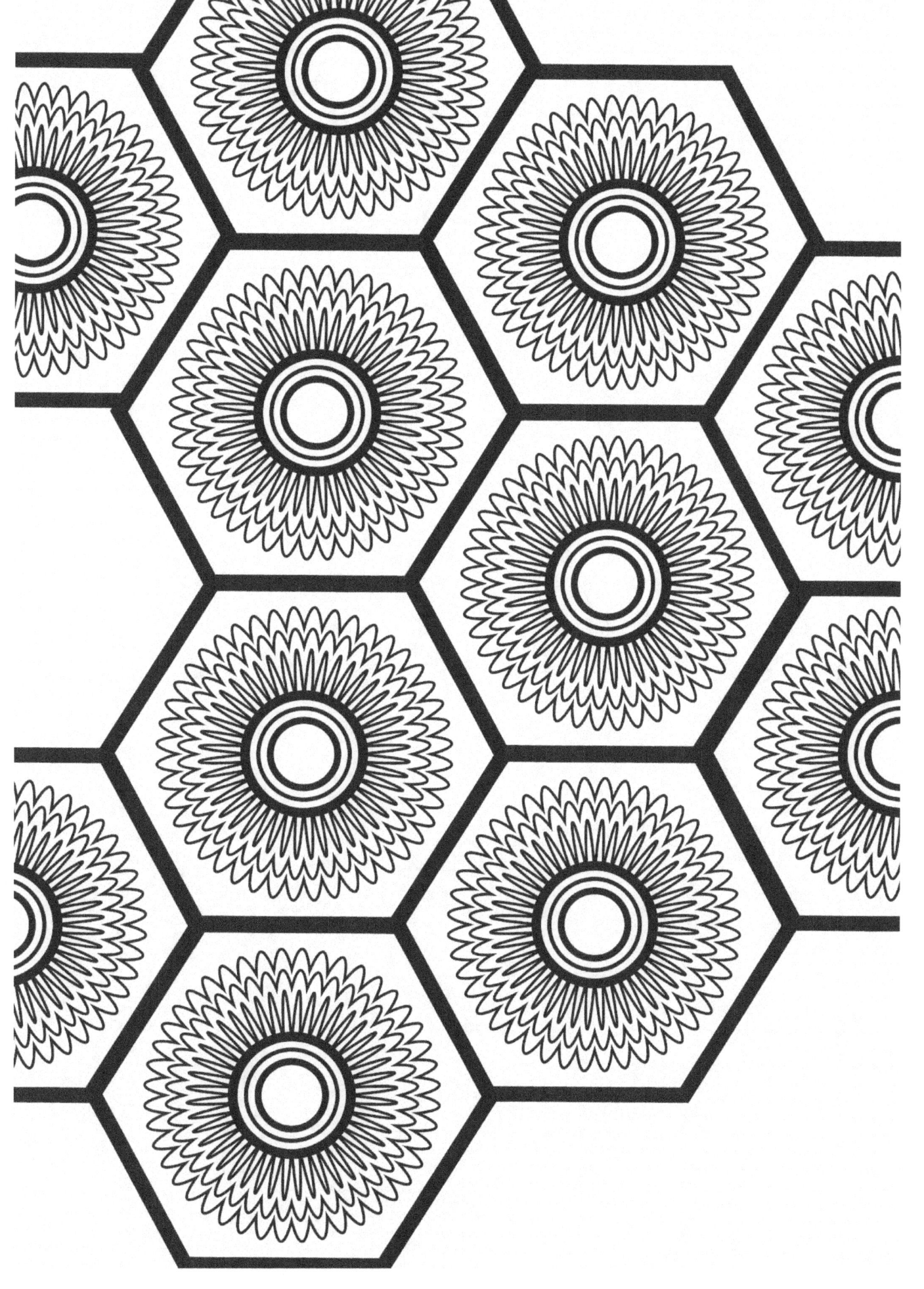

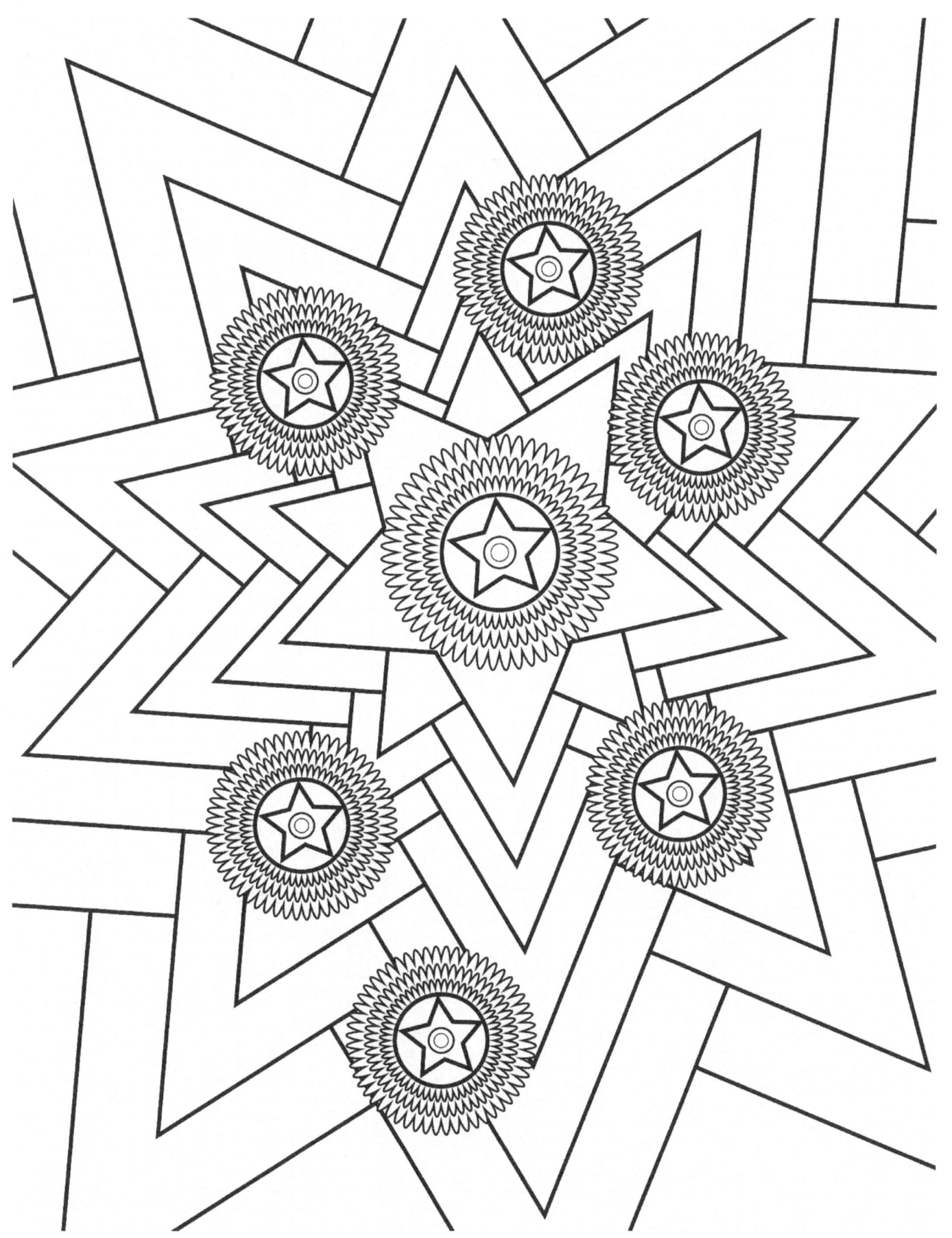

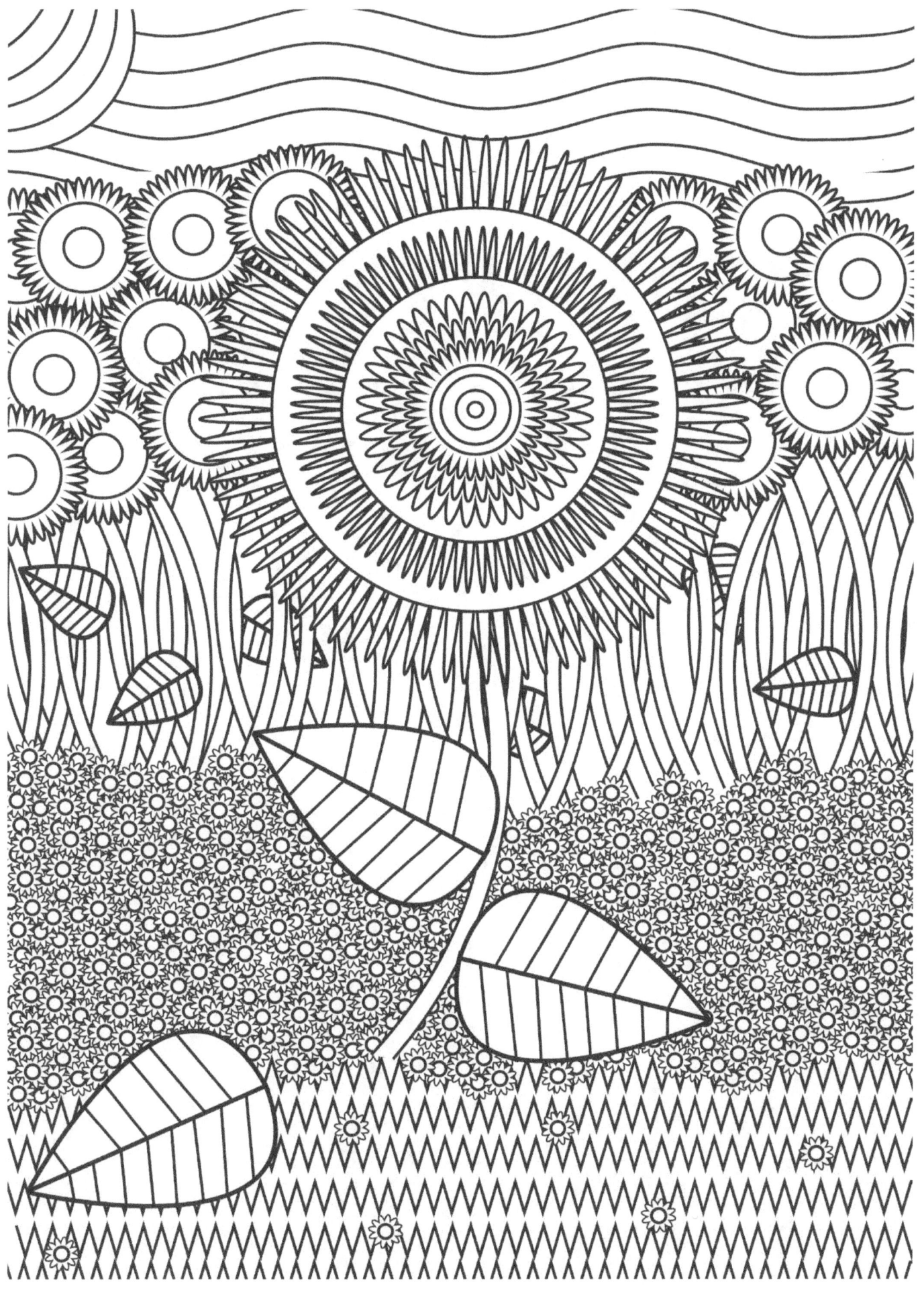

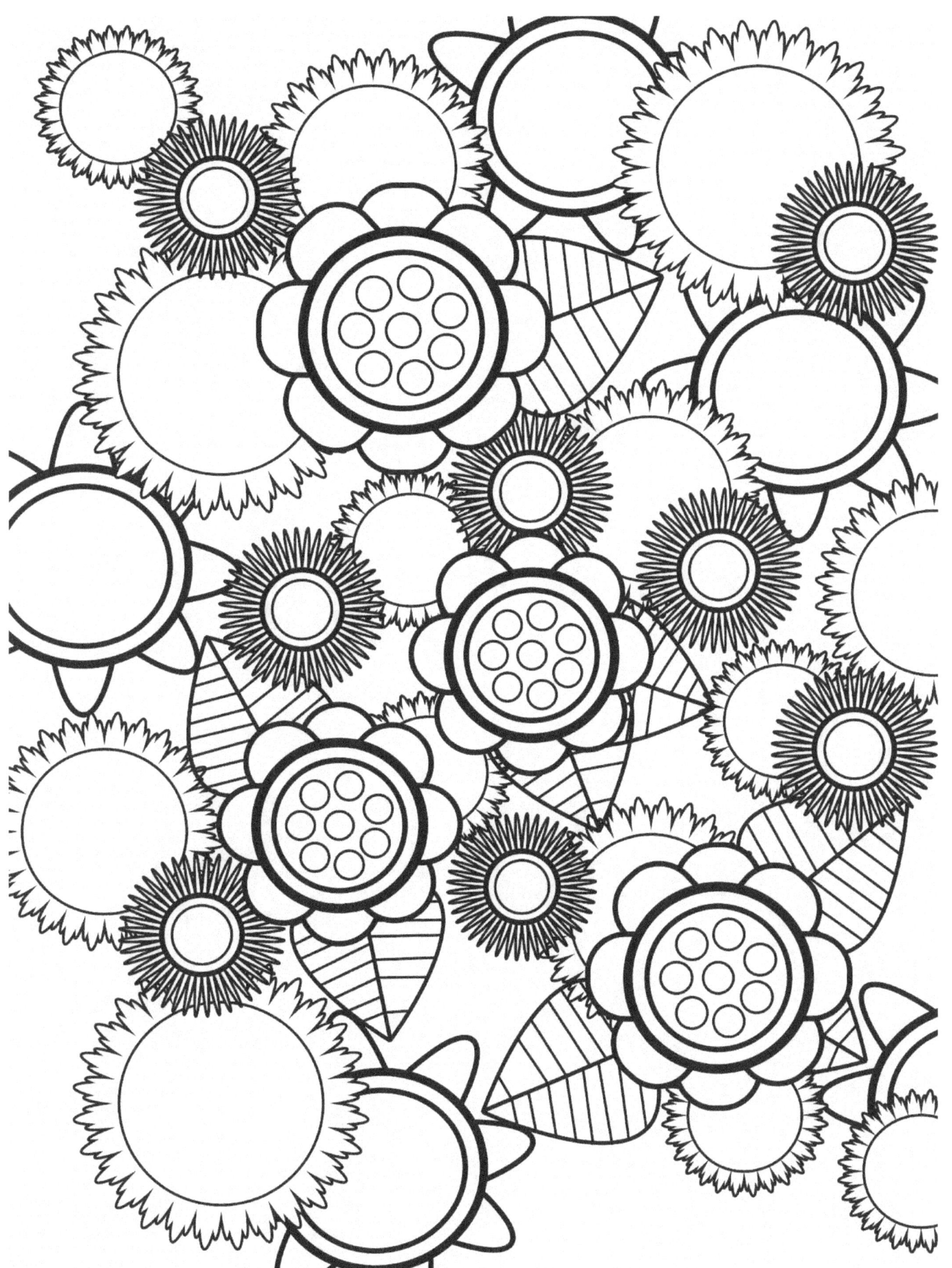

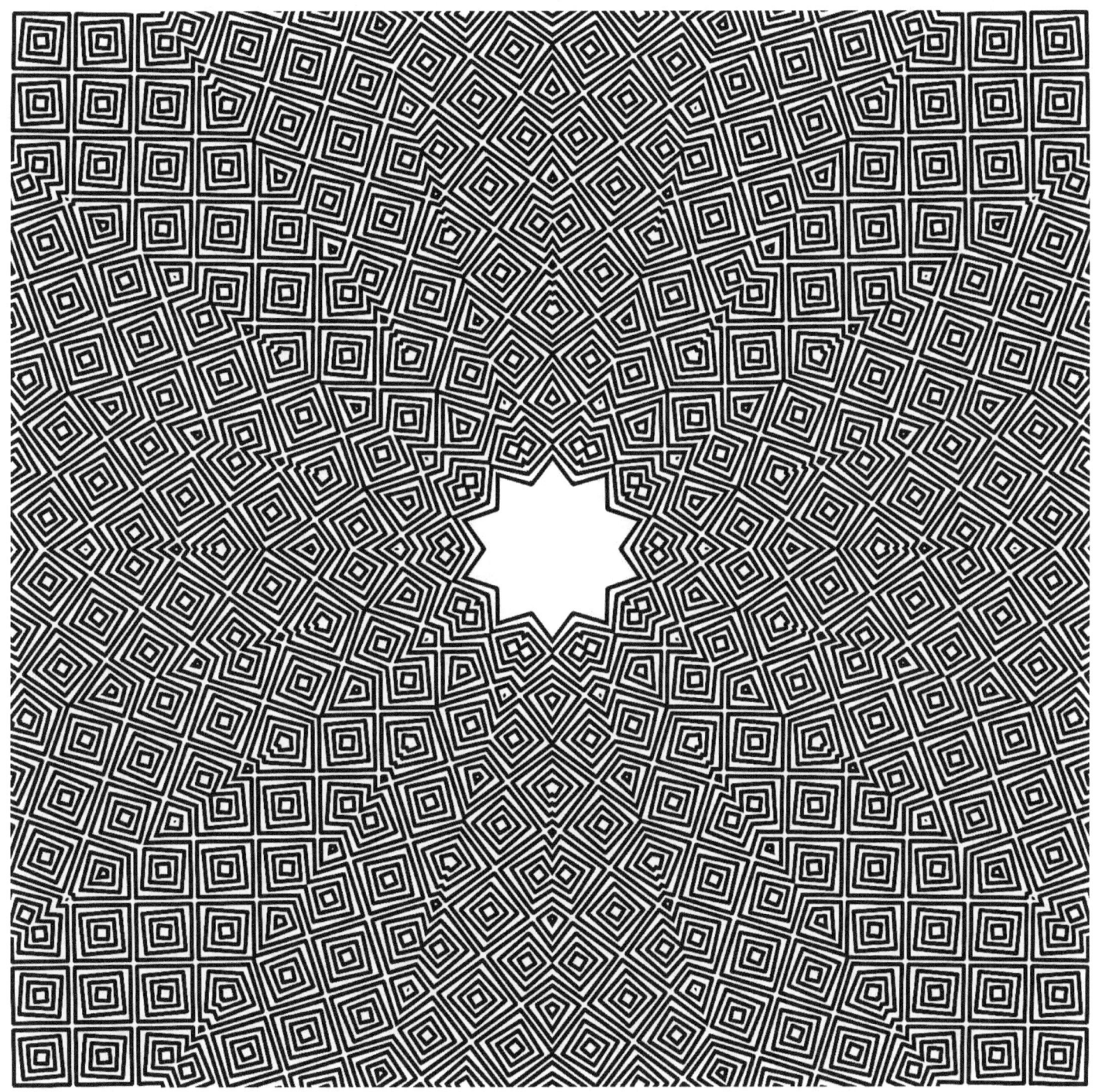

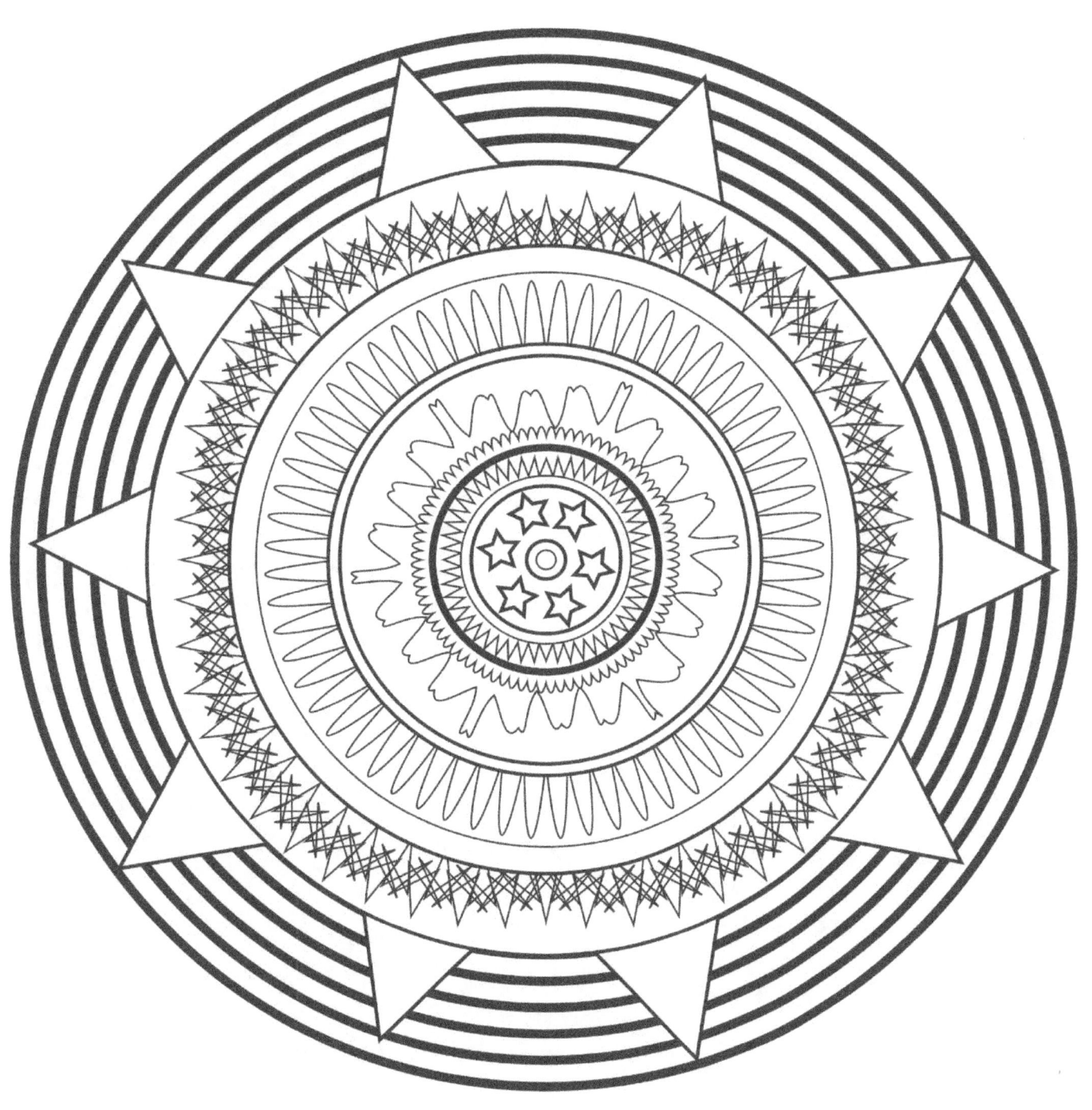

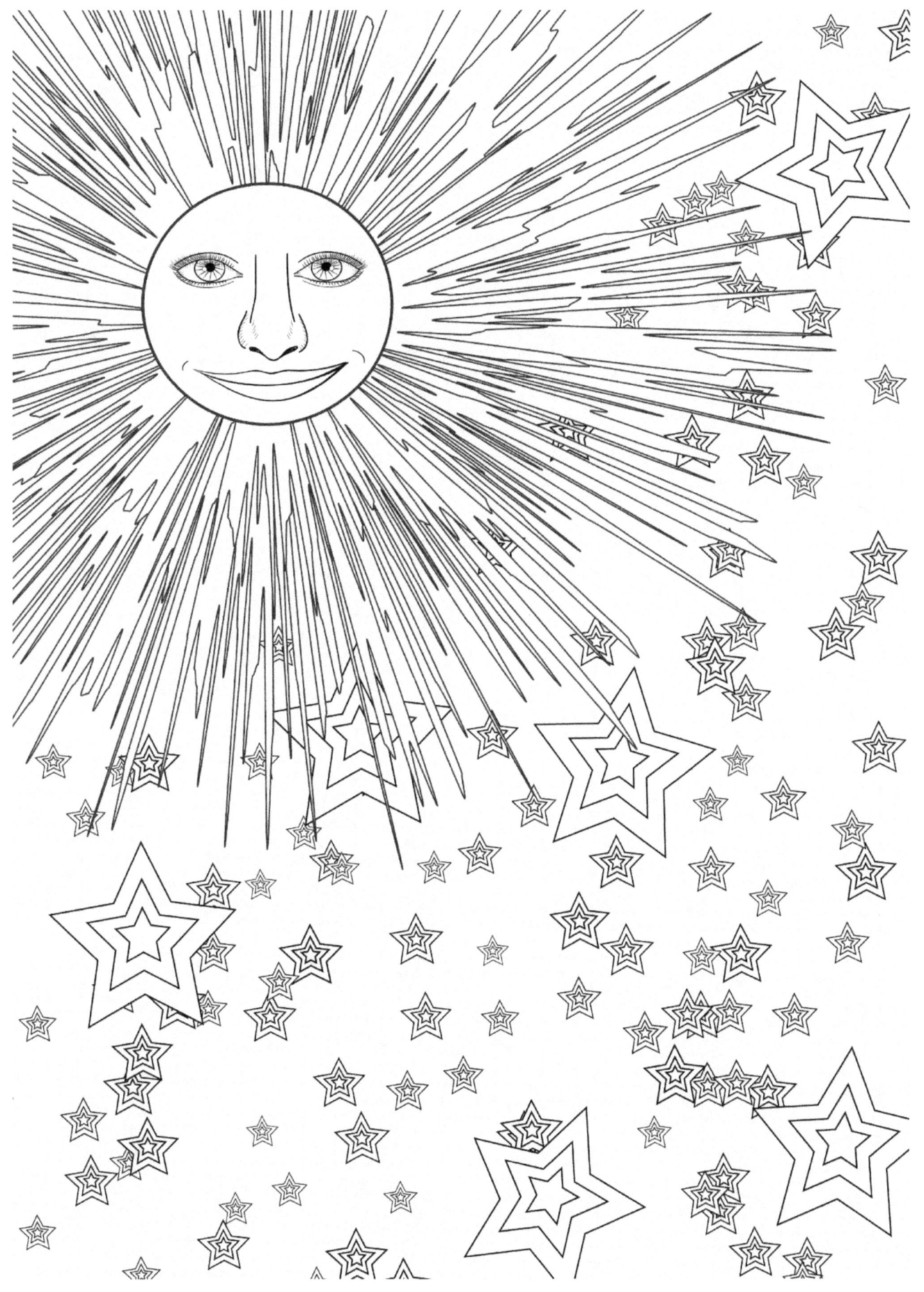

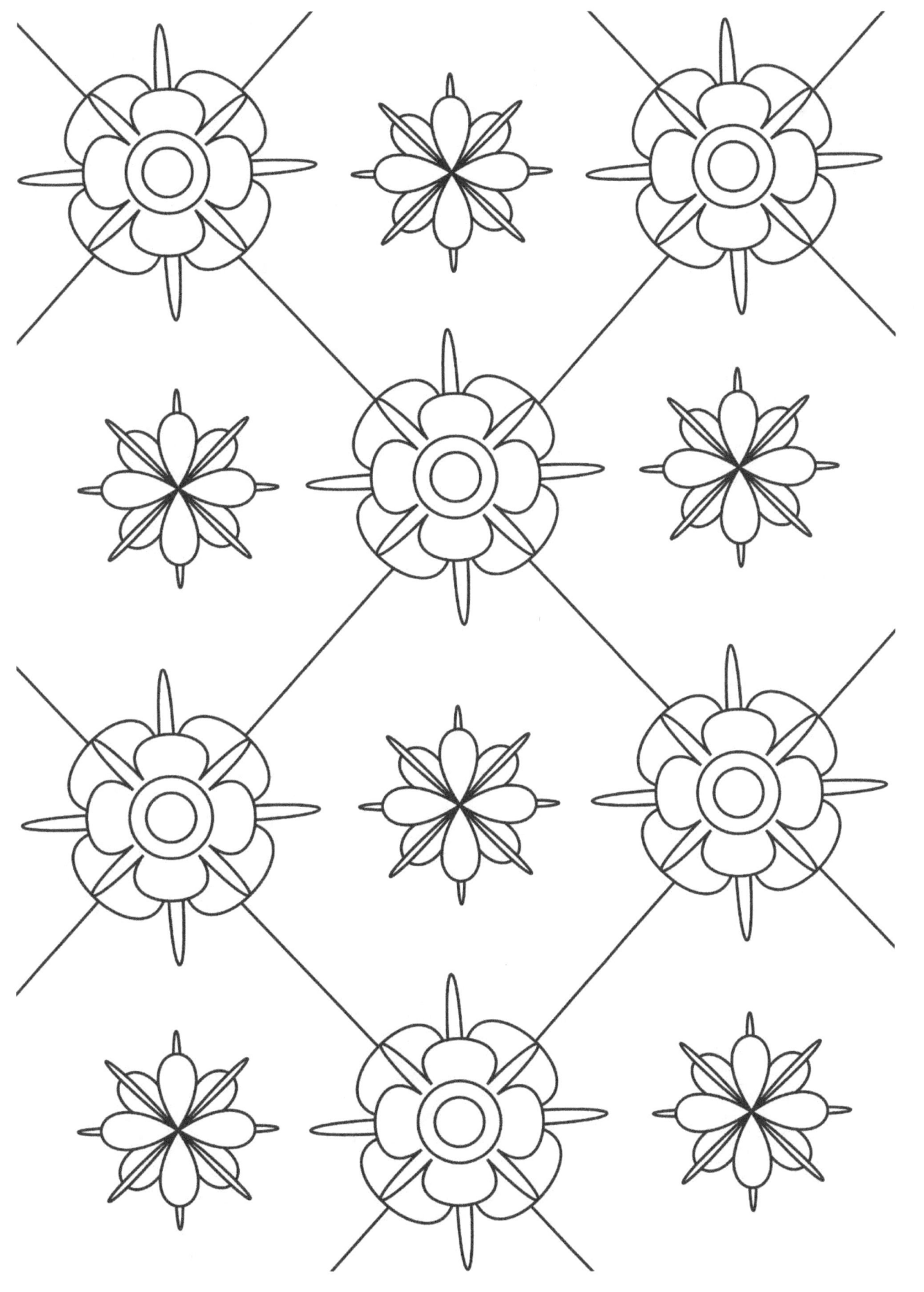

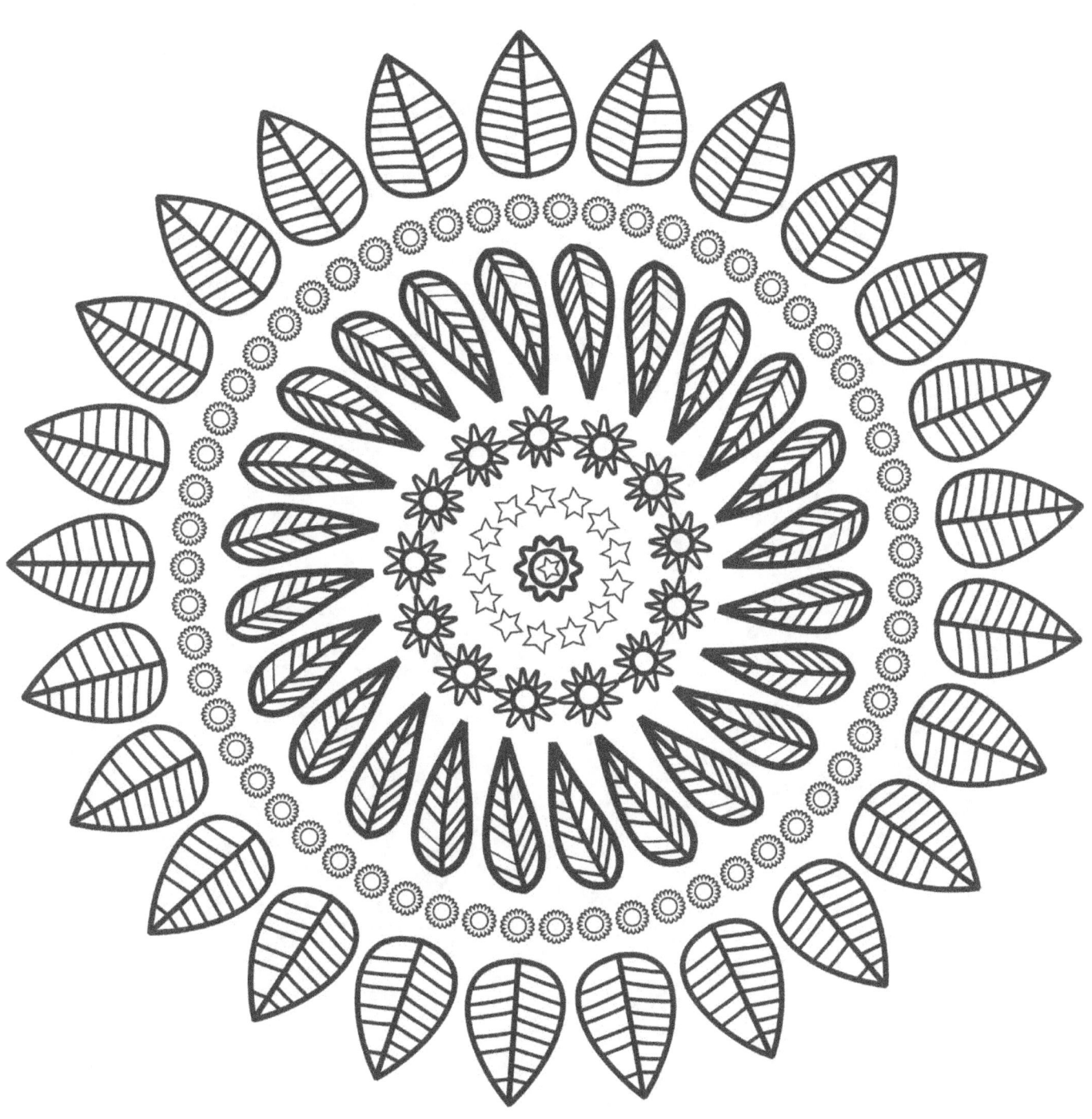

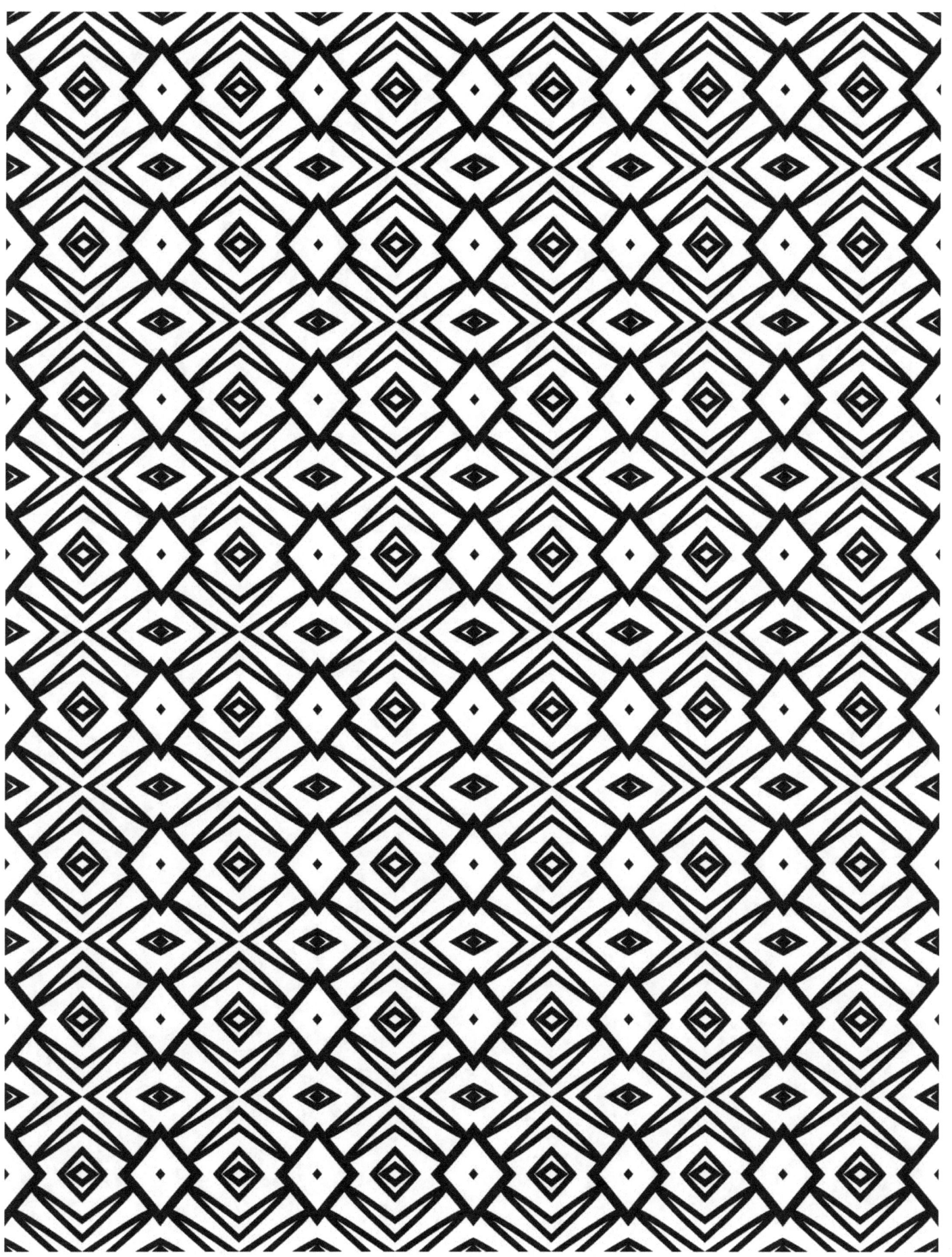

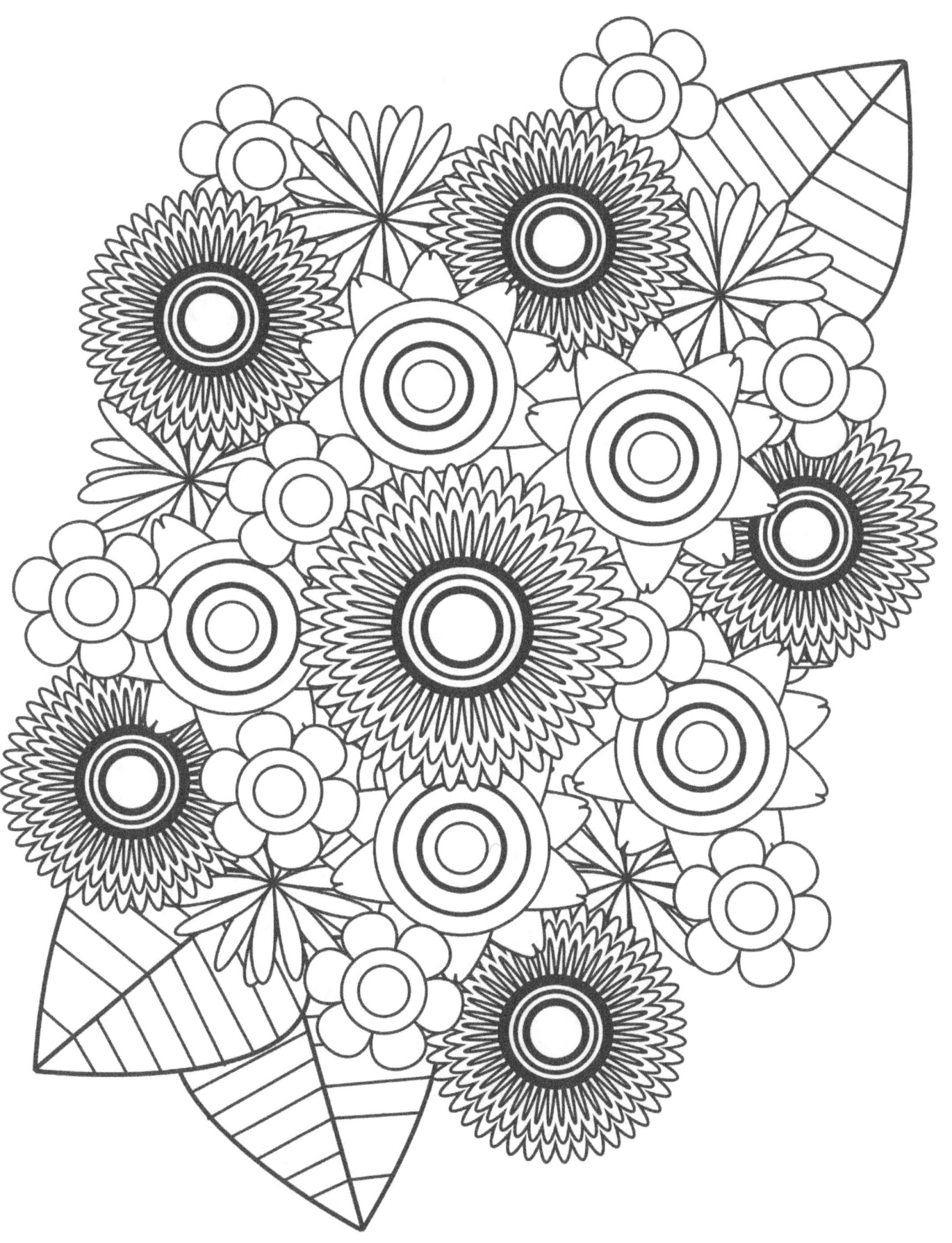

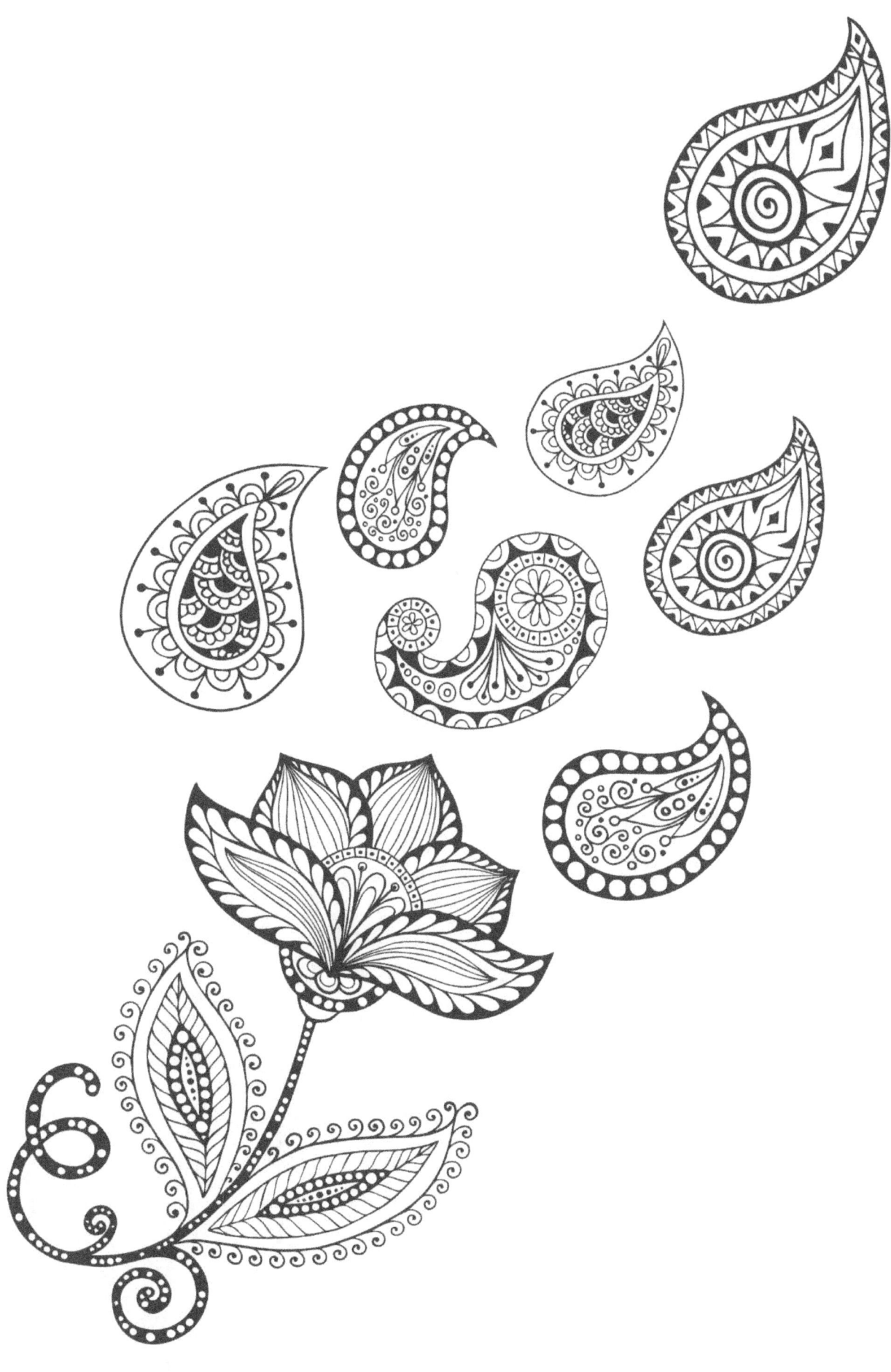

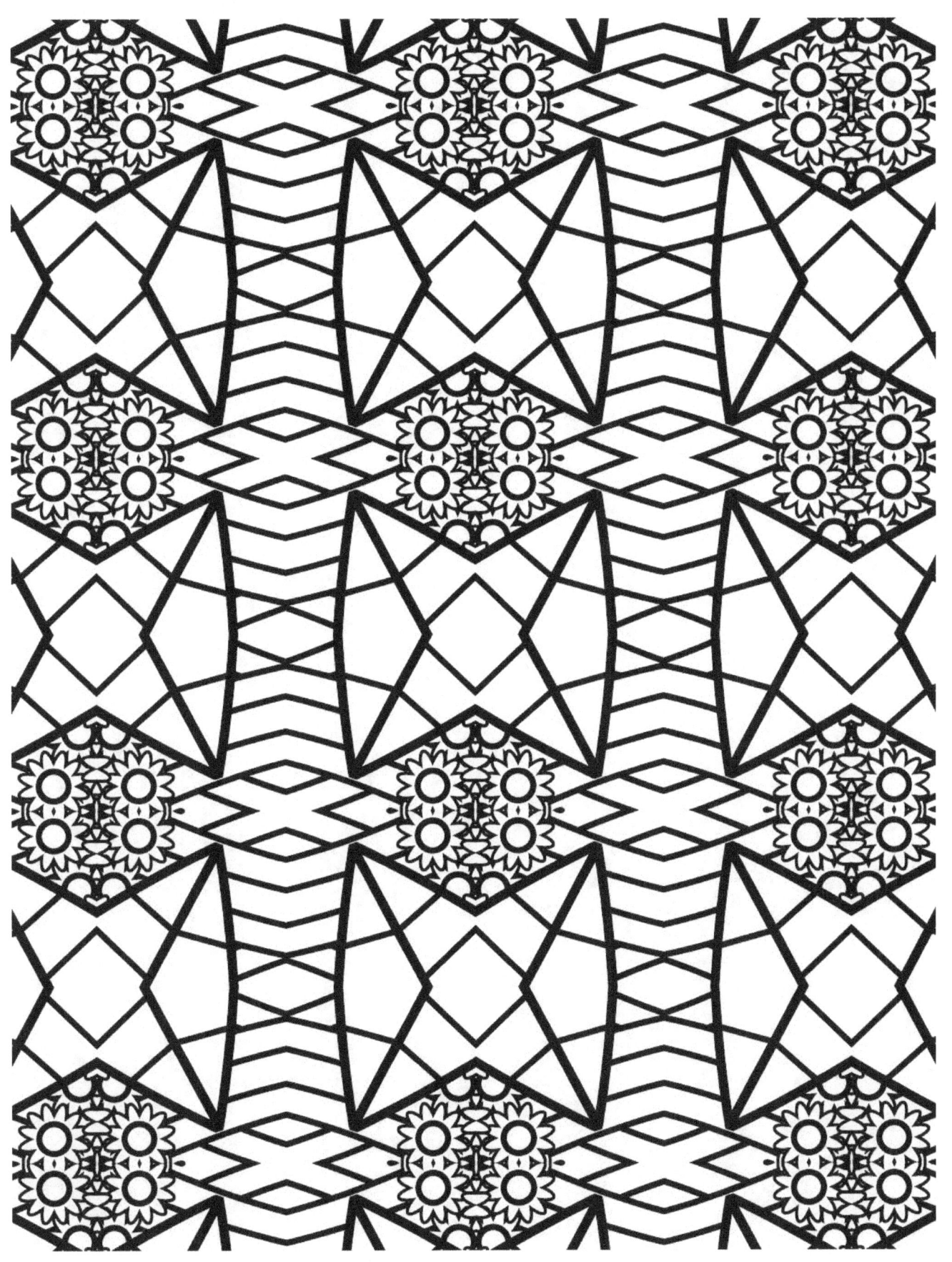

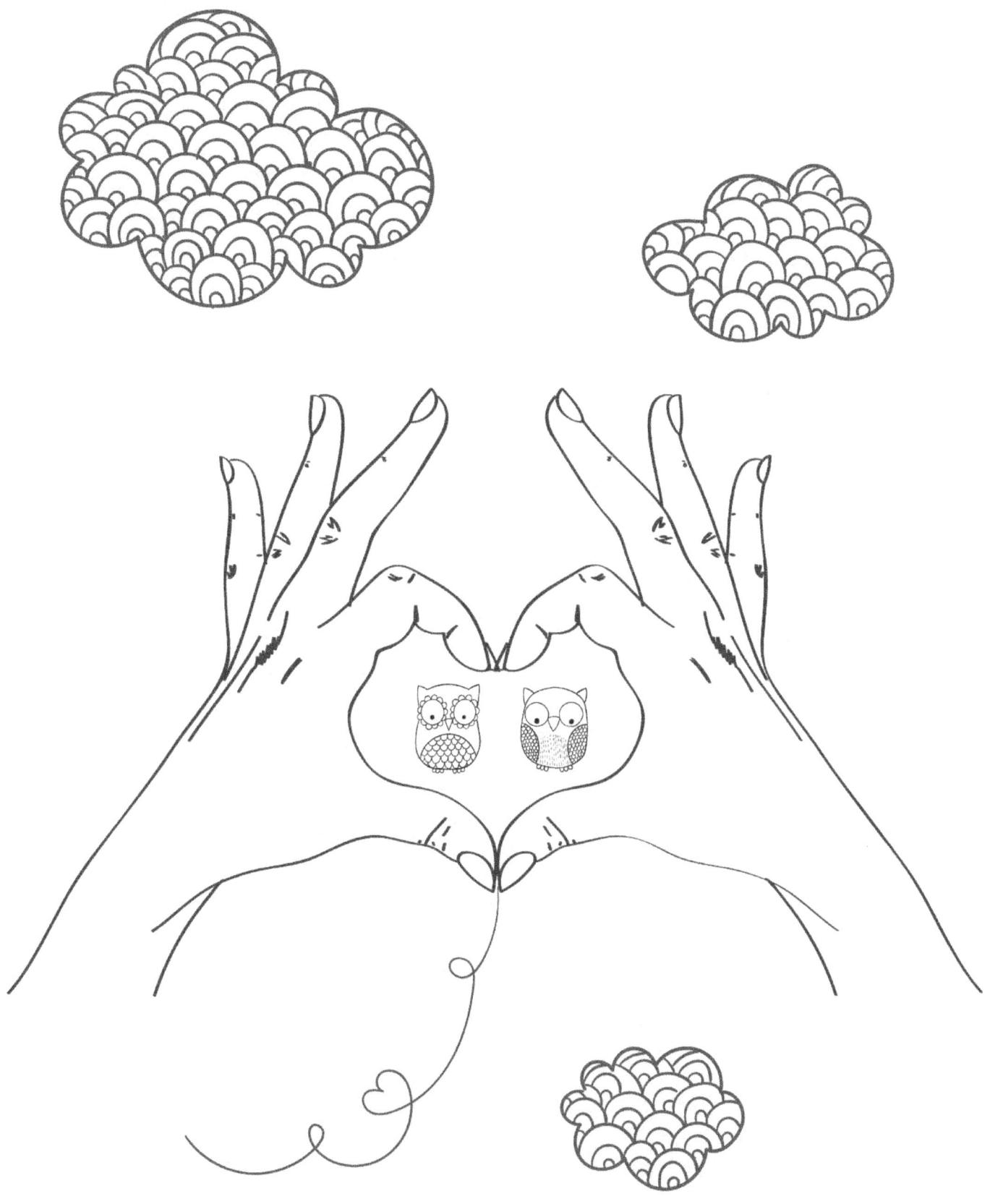

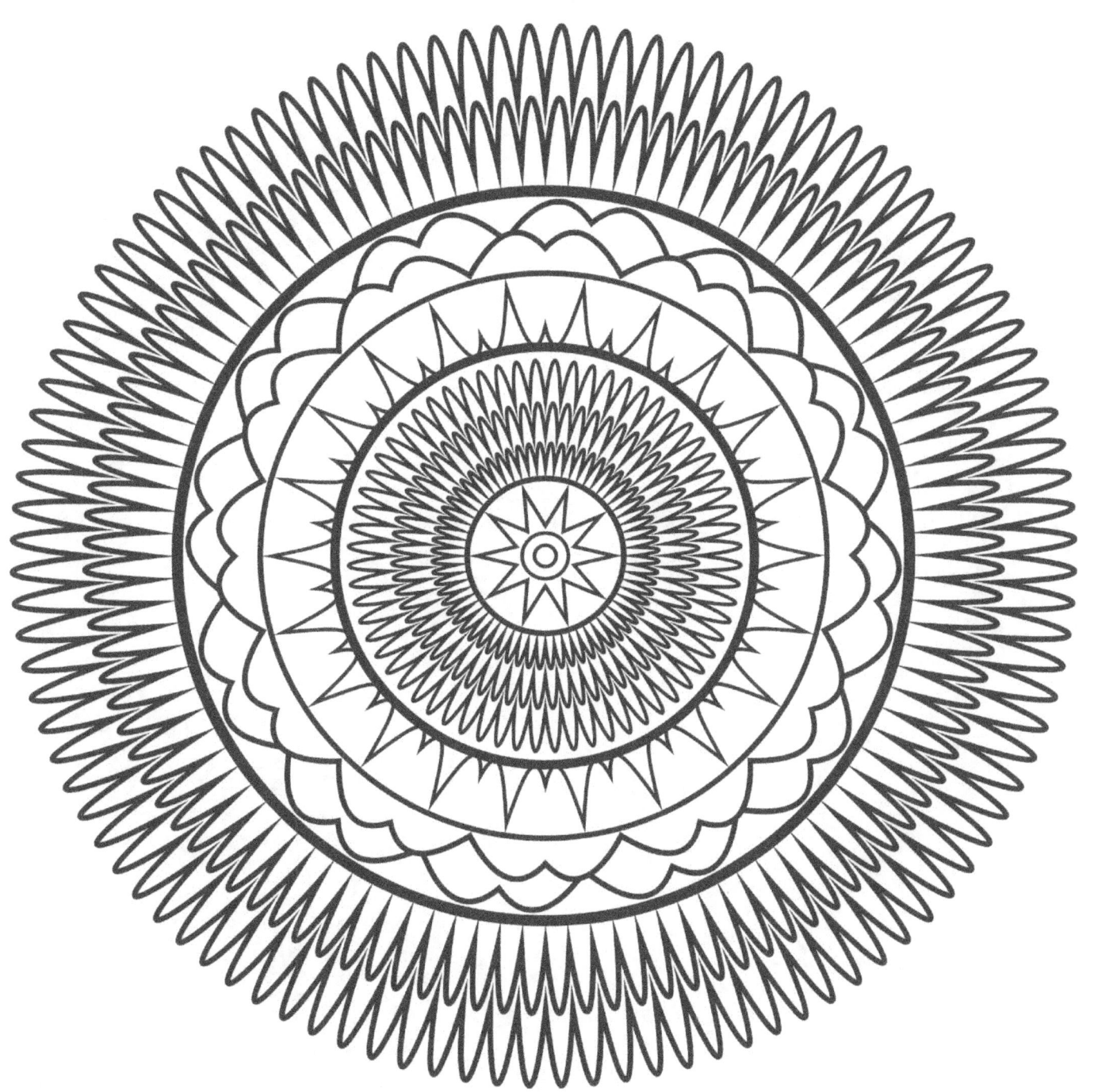

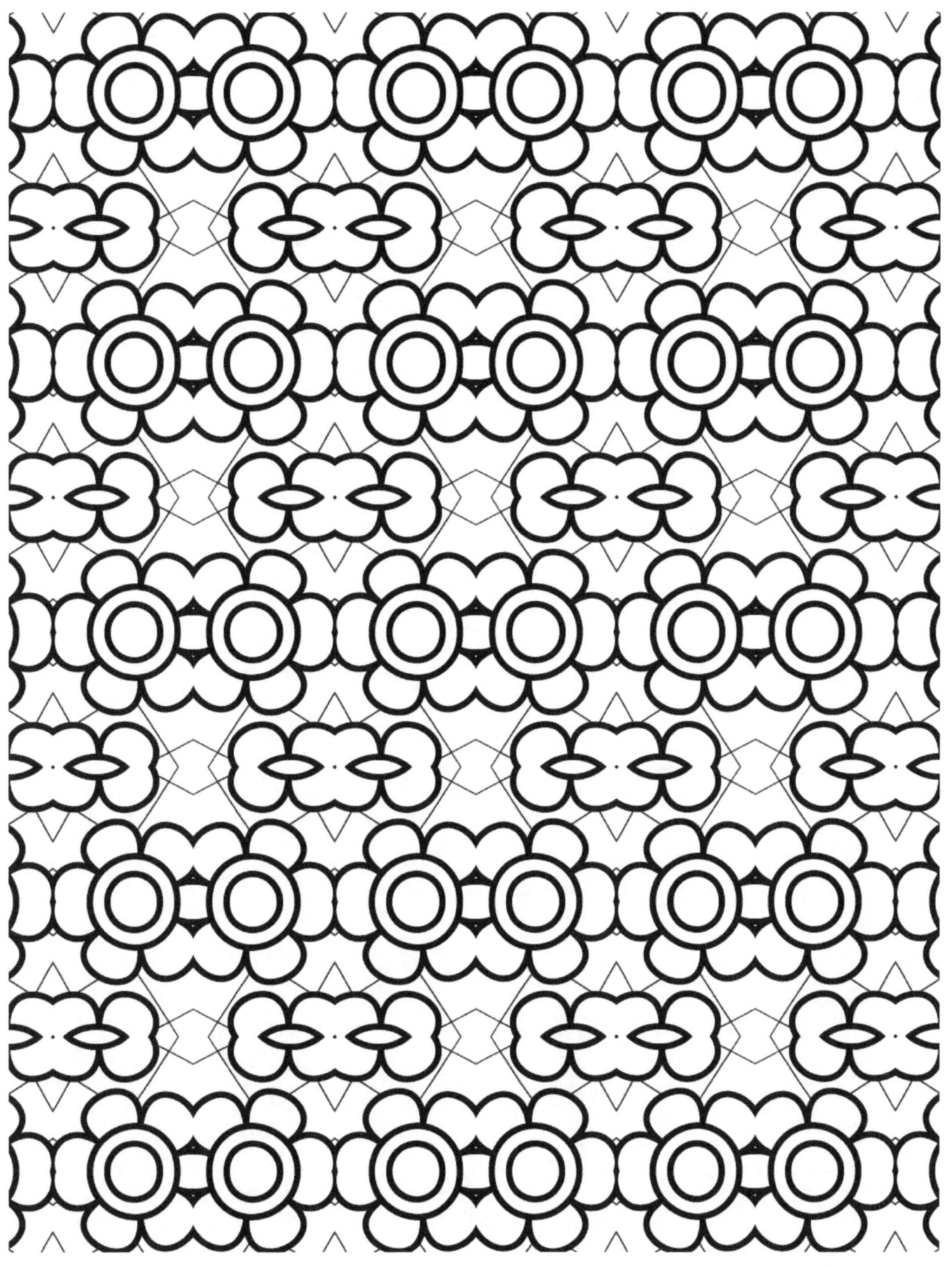

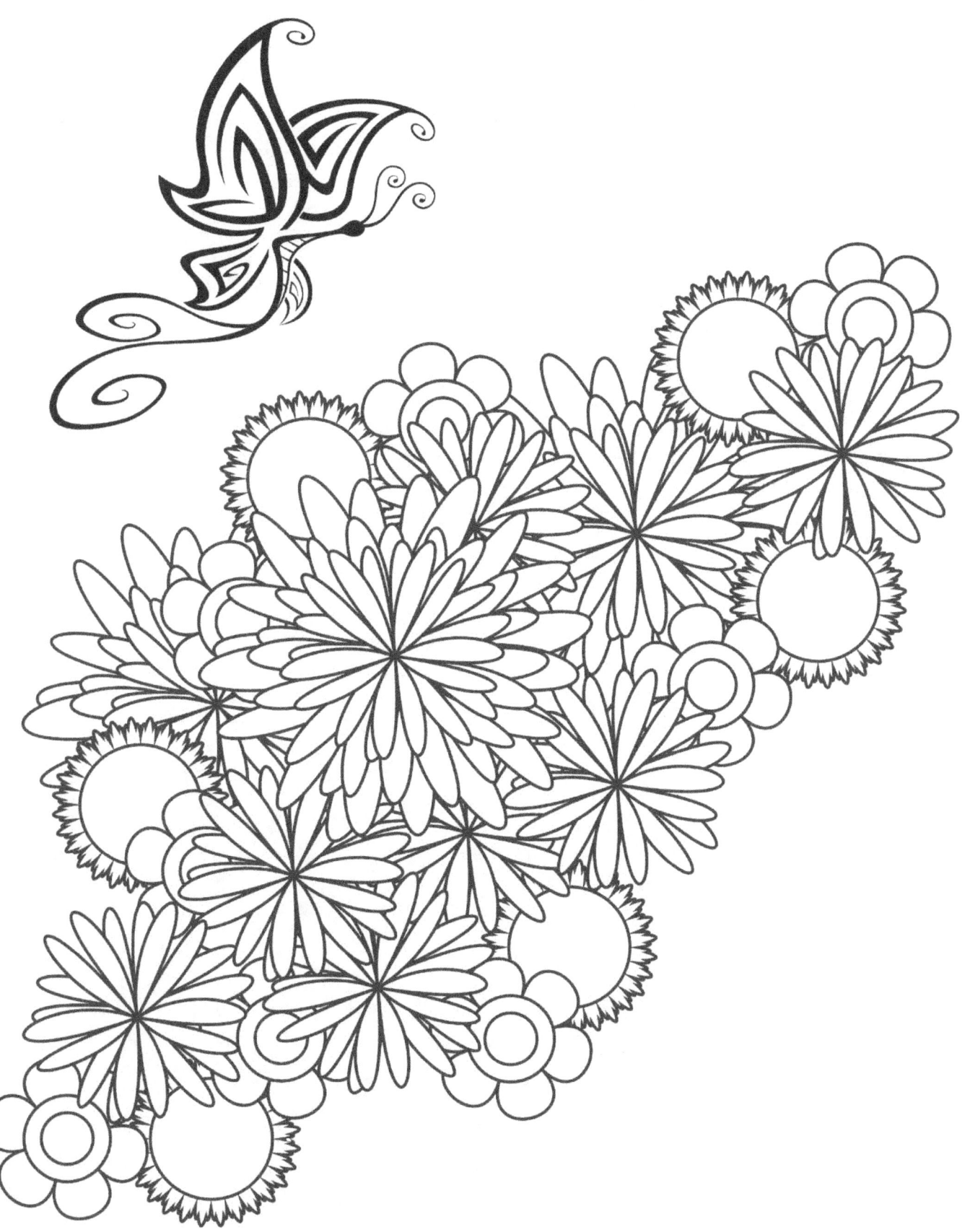

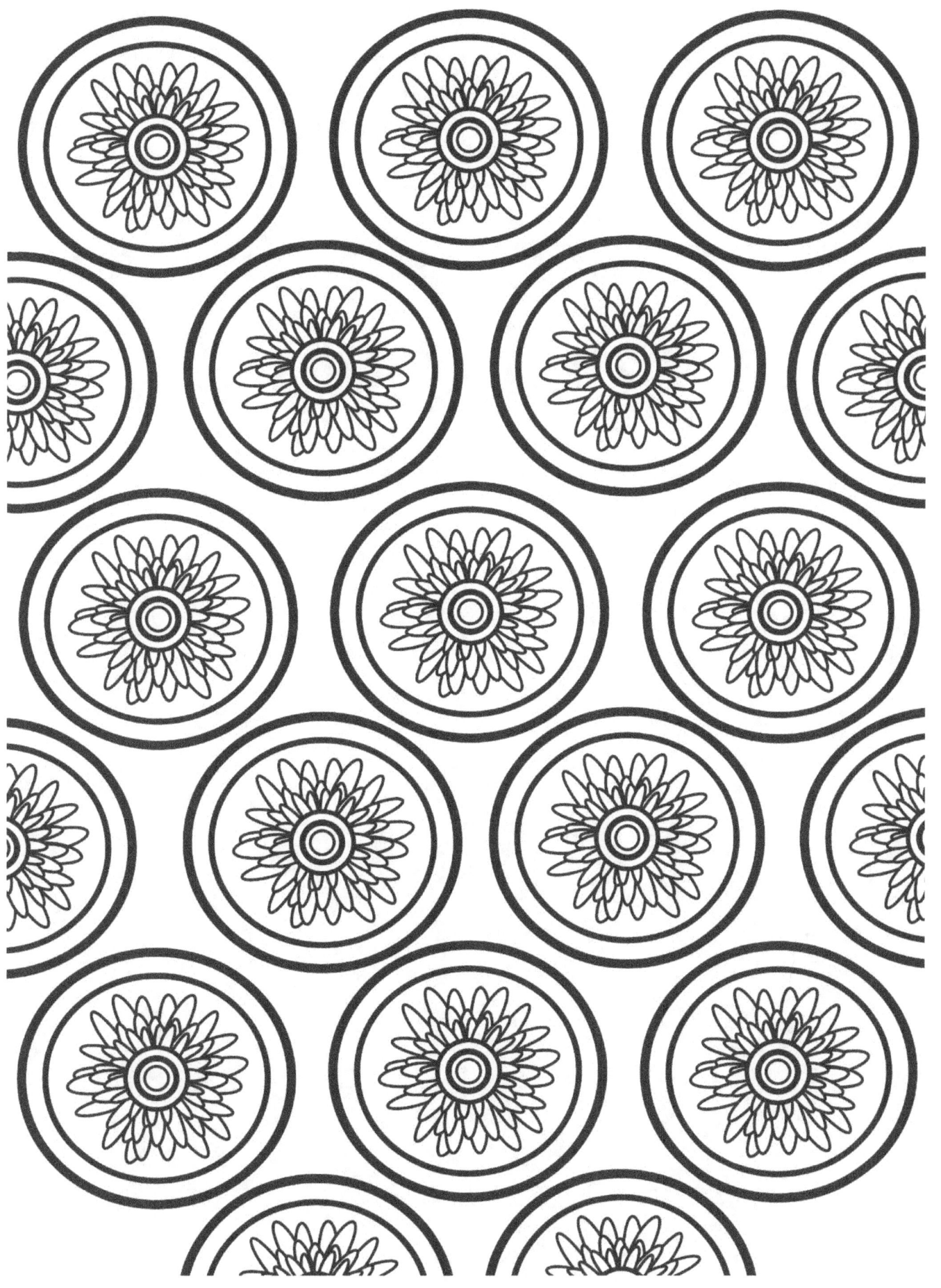

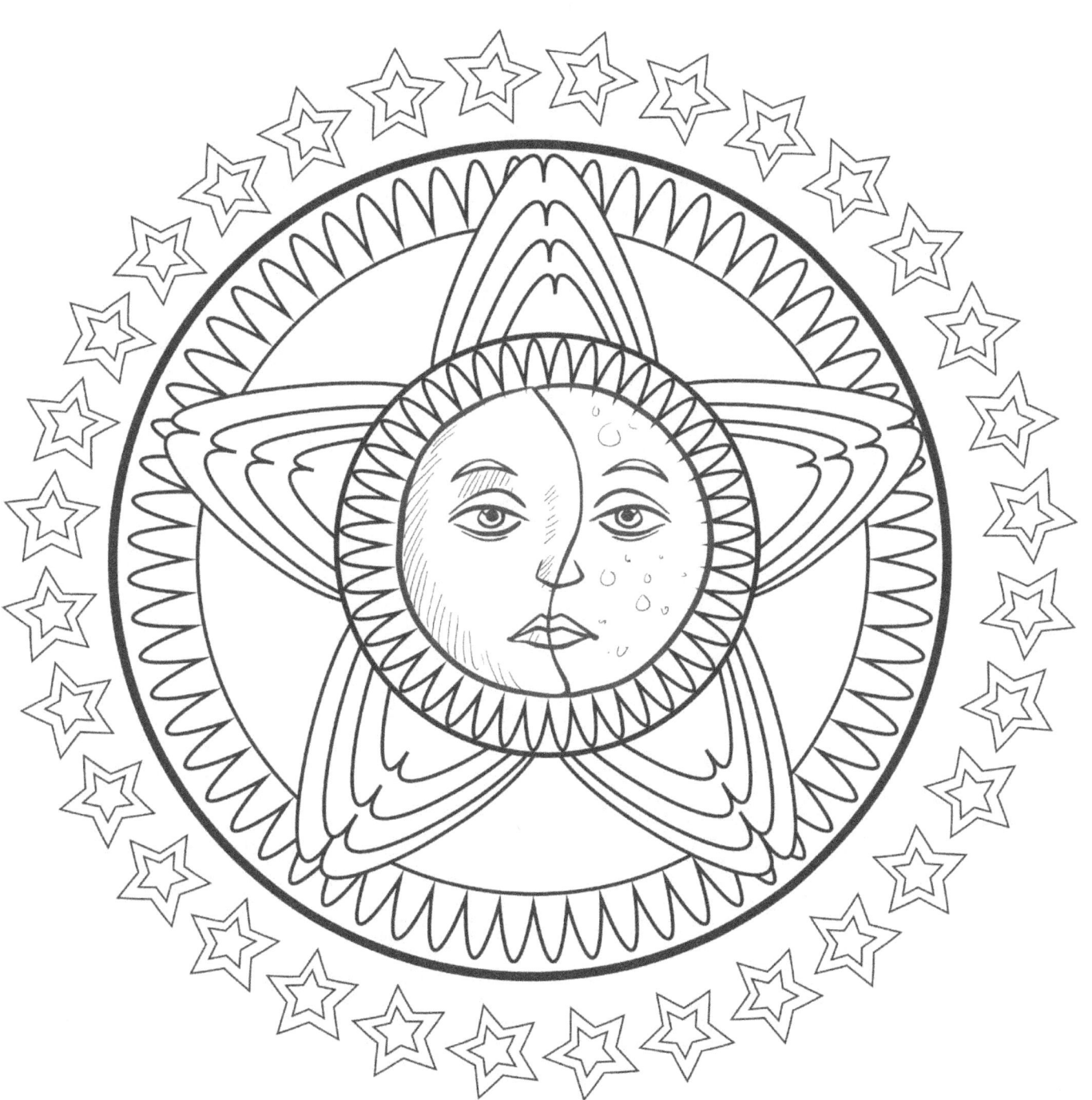

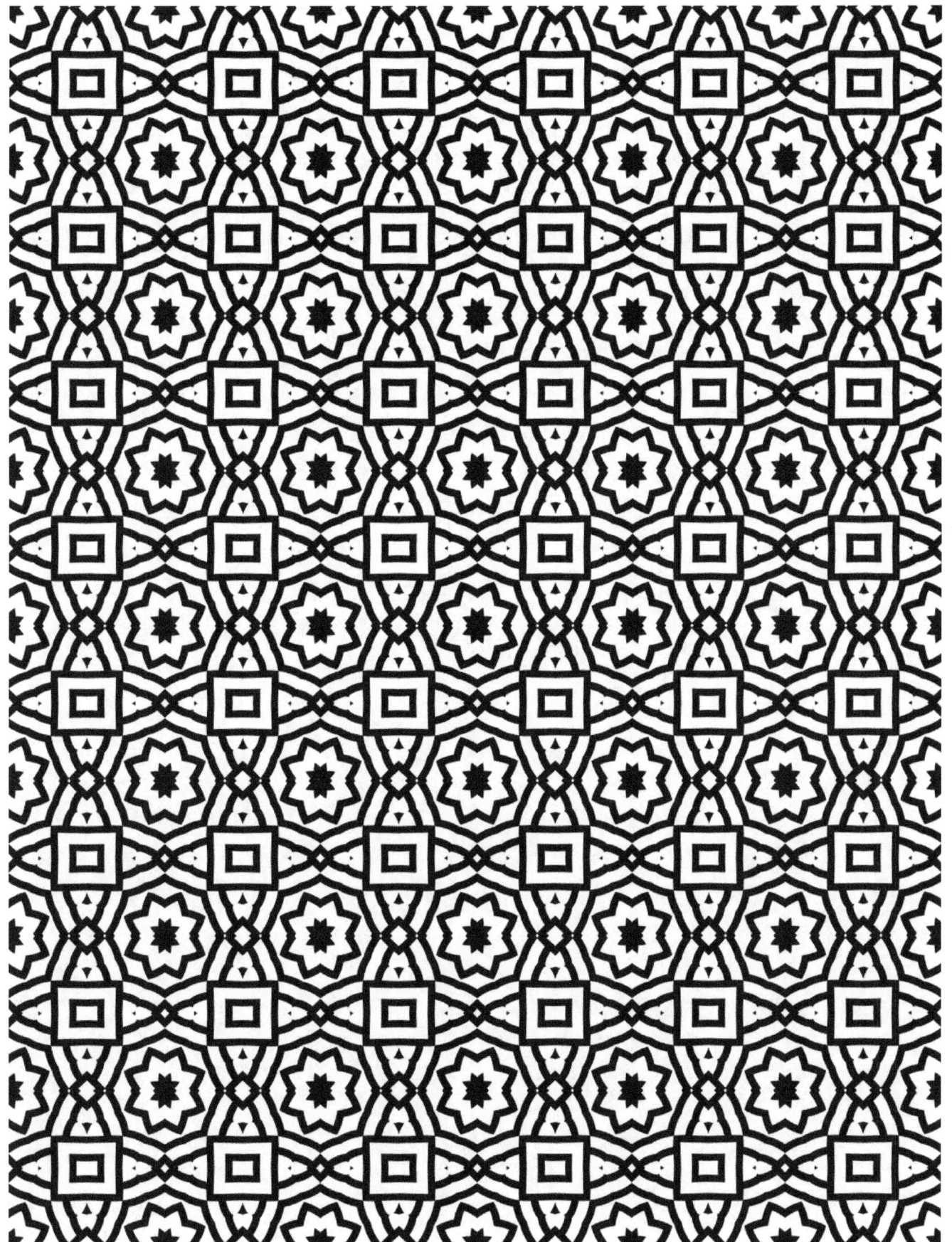

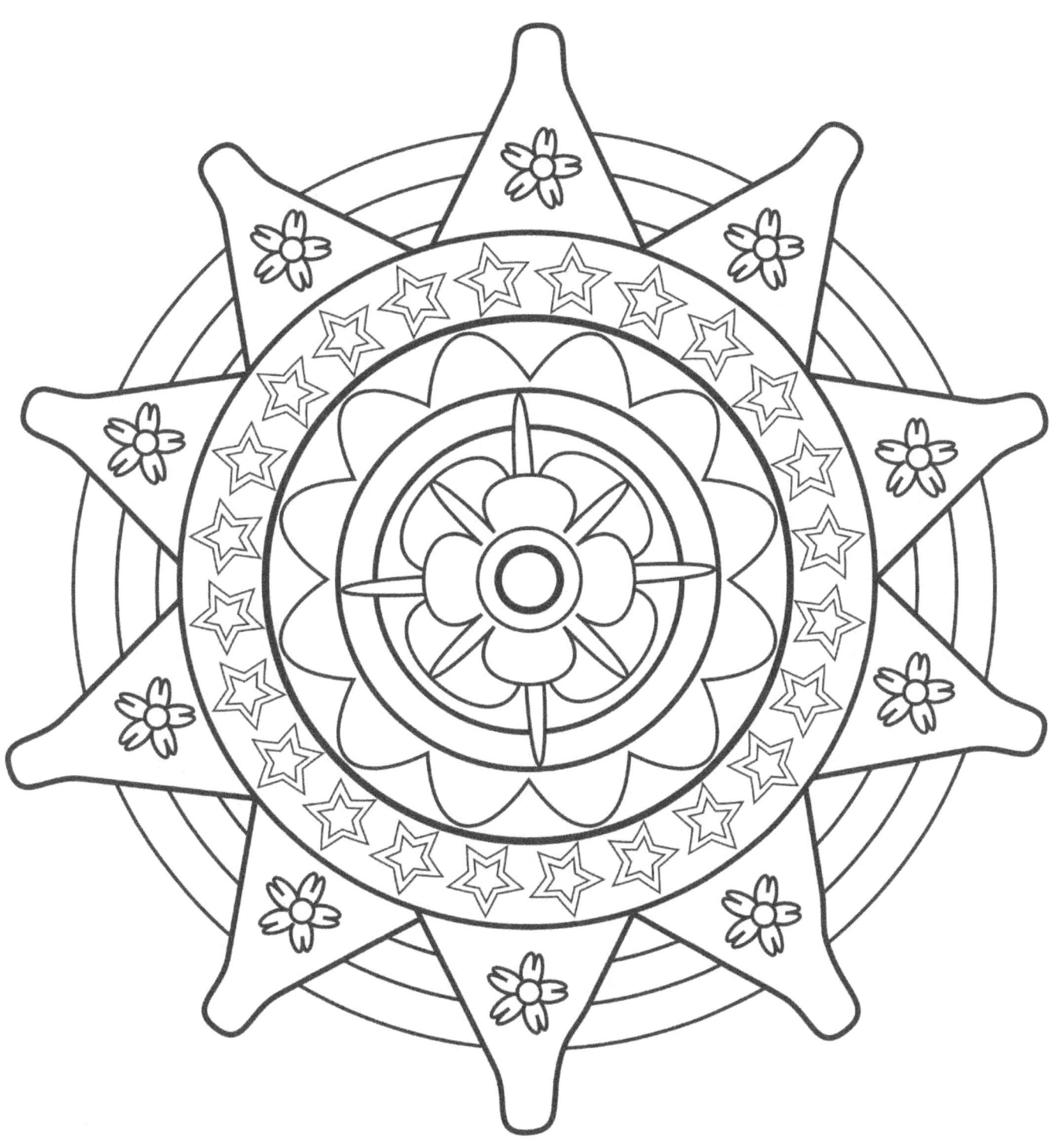

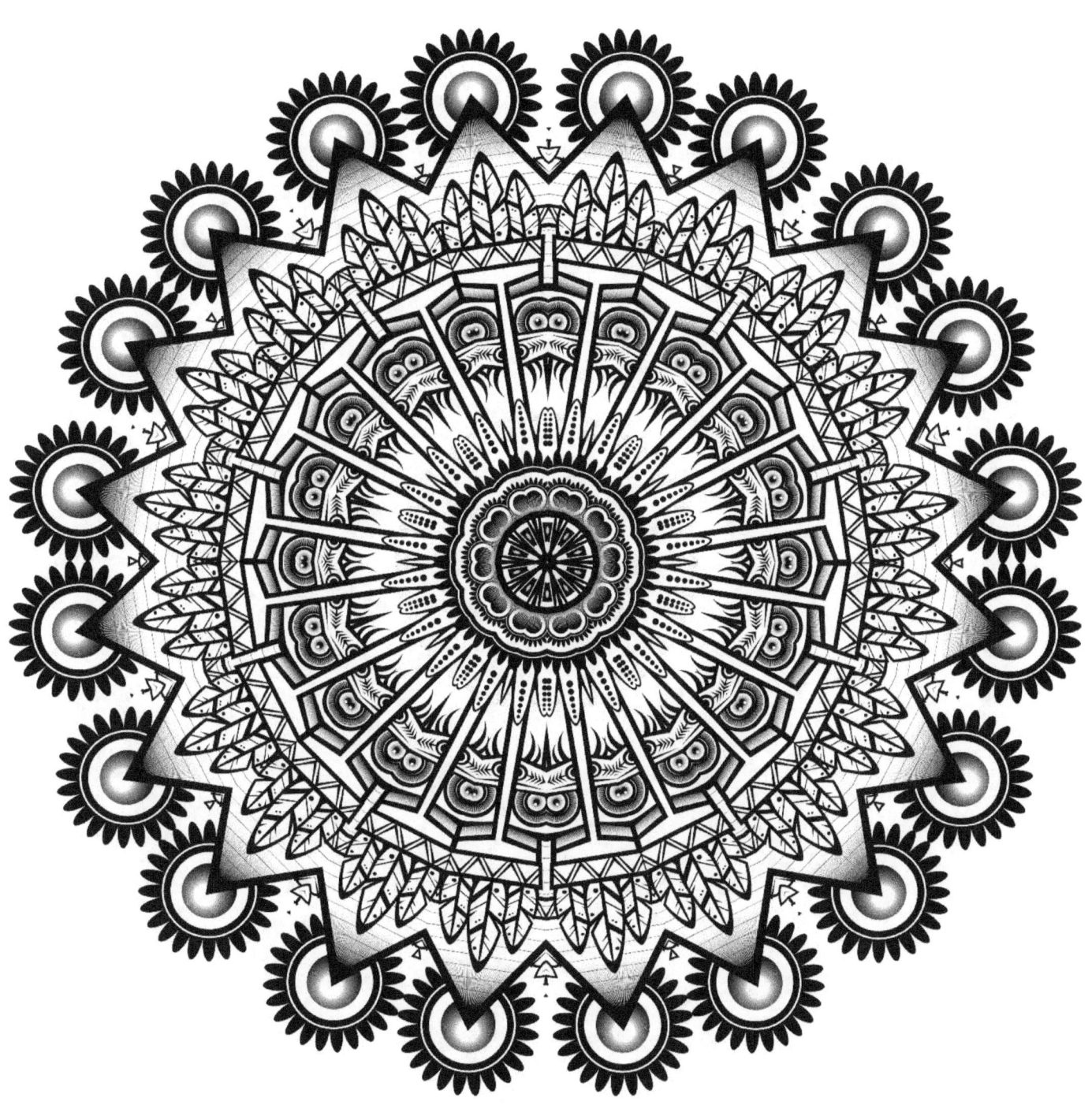

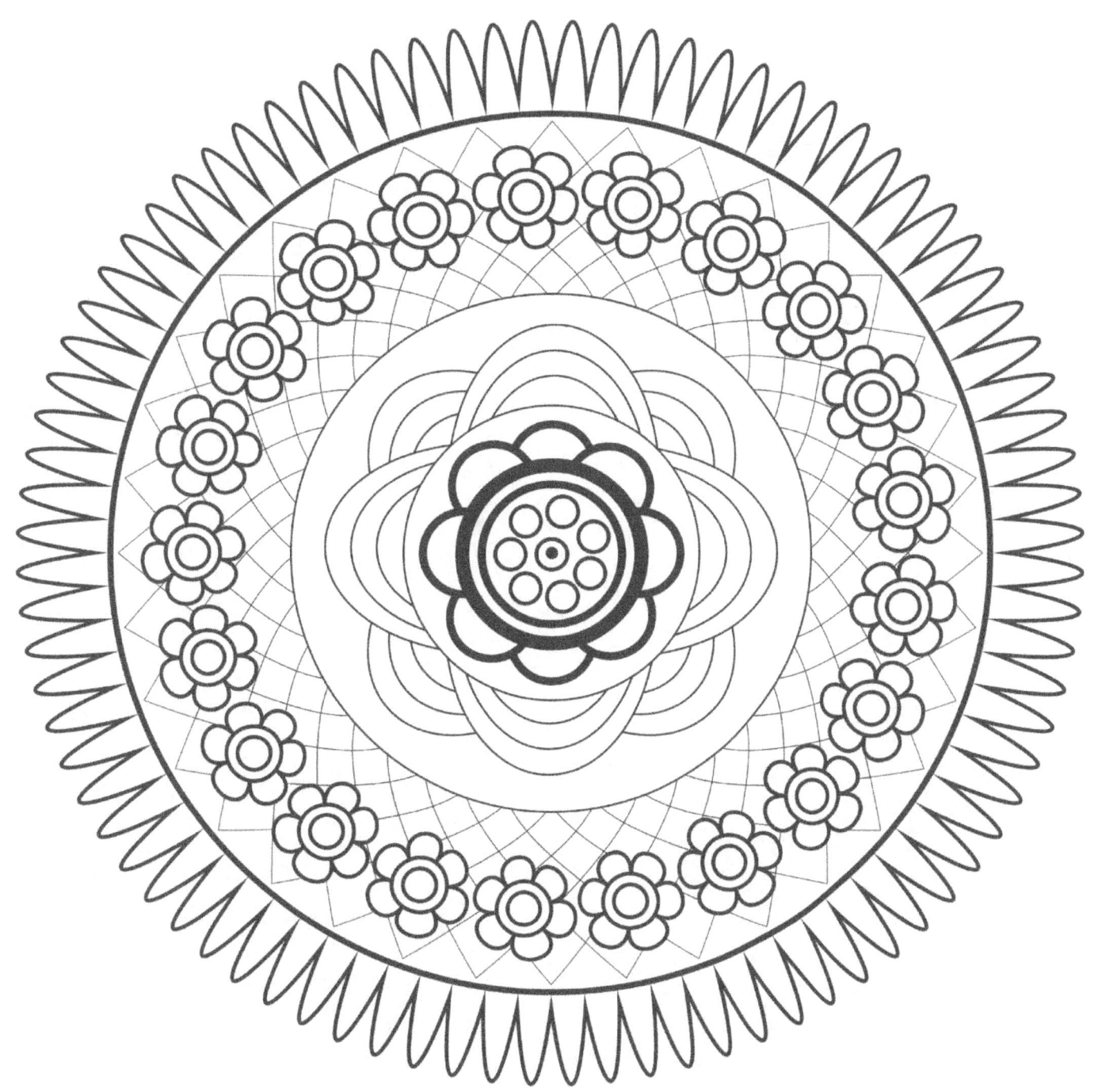

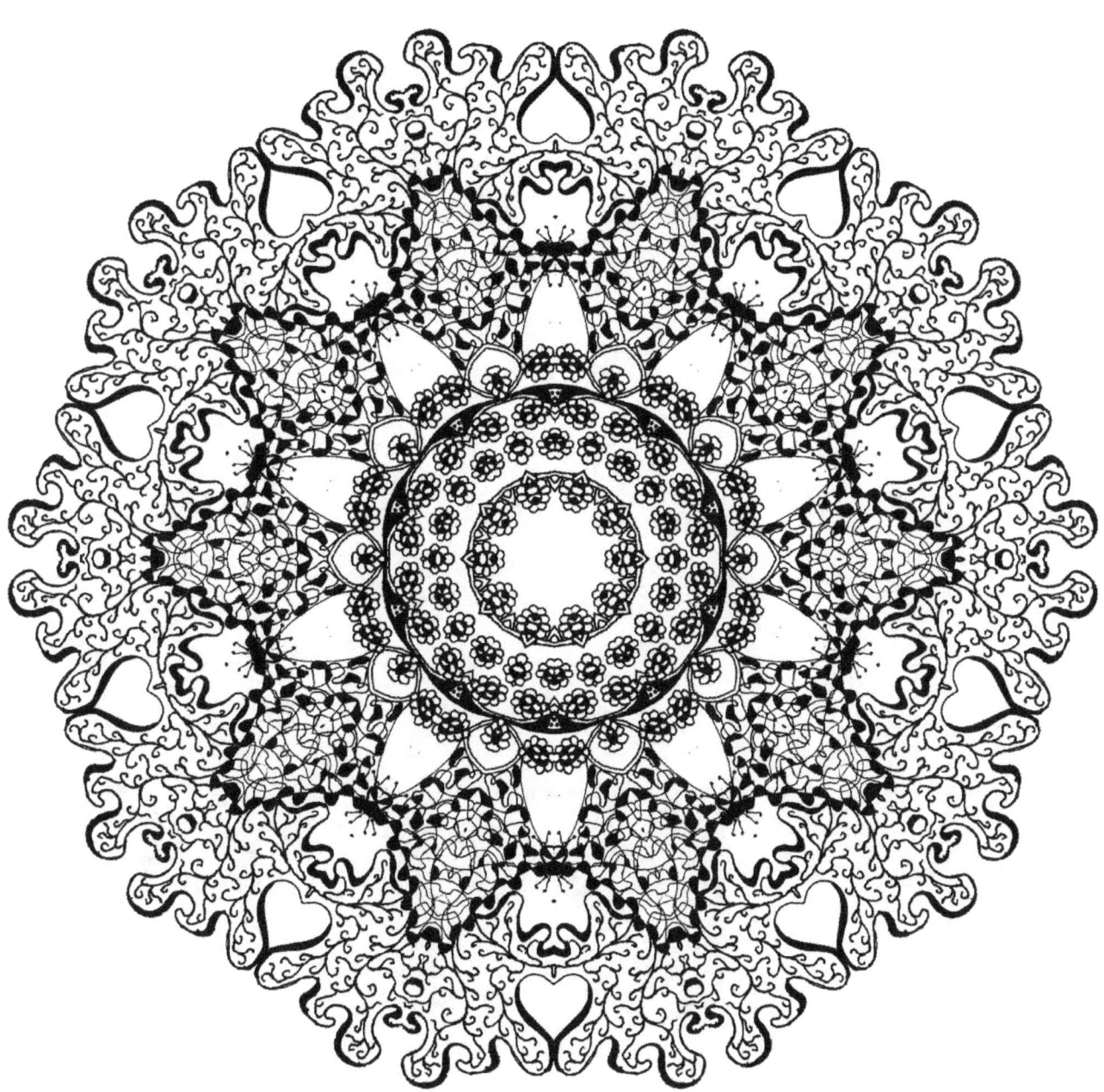

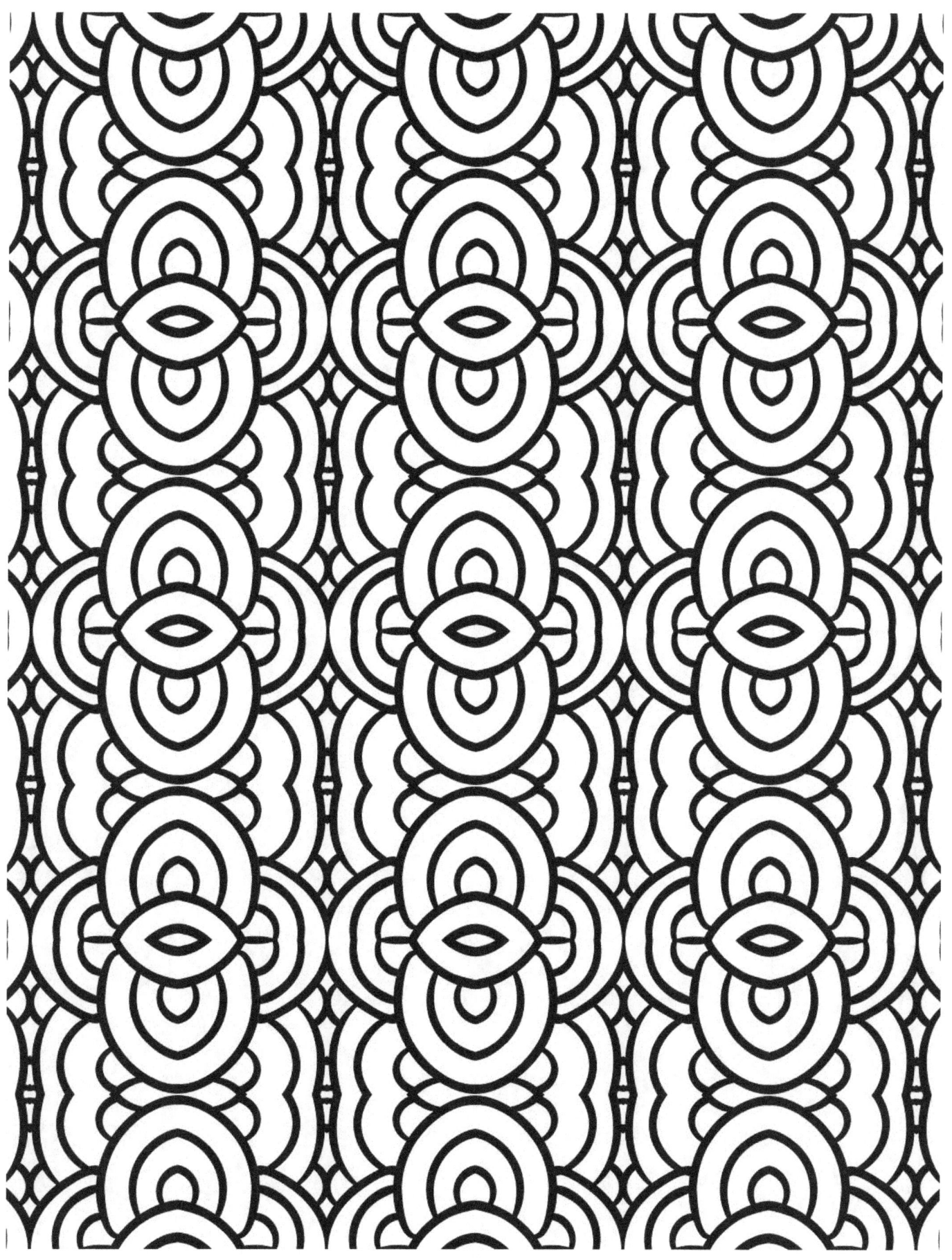